WORLD FAMOUS BUILDINGS

Burj Khalifa

by Alicia Z. Klepeis

BELLWETHER MEDIA • MINNEAPOLIS, MN

Blastoff! Readers are carefully developed by literacy experts to build reading stamina and move students toward fluency by combining standards-based content with developmentally appropriate text.

Level 1 provides the most support through repetition of high-frequency words, light text, predictable sentence patterns, and strong visual support.

Level 2 offers early readers a bit more challenge through varied sentences, increased text load, and text-supportive special features.

Level 3 advances early-fluent readers toward fluency through increased text load, less reliance on photos, advancing concepts, longer sentences, and more complex special features.

★ **Blastoff! Universe**

Reading Level

Blastoff! Beginners — Grade K

Blastoff! Readers — Grades 1–3

Blastoff! Discovery — Grade 4

This edition first published in 2026 by Bellwether Media, Inc.

Library of Congress Cataloging-in-Publication Data

LC record for Burj Khalifa available at: https://lccn.loc.gov/2025018597

Editor: Megan Borgert-Spaniol   Series Designer: Chase Demmin

Printed in the United States of America, North Mankato, MN.

Table of Contents

What Is the Burj Khalifa?

The Burj Khalifa is one of the world's tallest buildings. It is in Dubai, United Arab Emirates (UAE).

Burj means "tower" in Arabic. Khalifa is the last name of a past UAE president.

Building Location

The Burj Khalifa has apartments. It also has offices.

restaurant

Visitors go to hotels and restaurants. They go to the **observation decks**, too.

History of the Burj Khalifa

The Burj Khalifa was made to grow **tourism**. It was built from 2004 to 2010.

The **architect** Adrian Smith **designed** the tower. William F. Baker was the lead **engineer**.

Adrian Smith

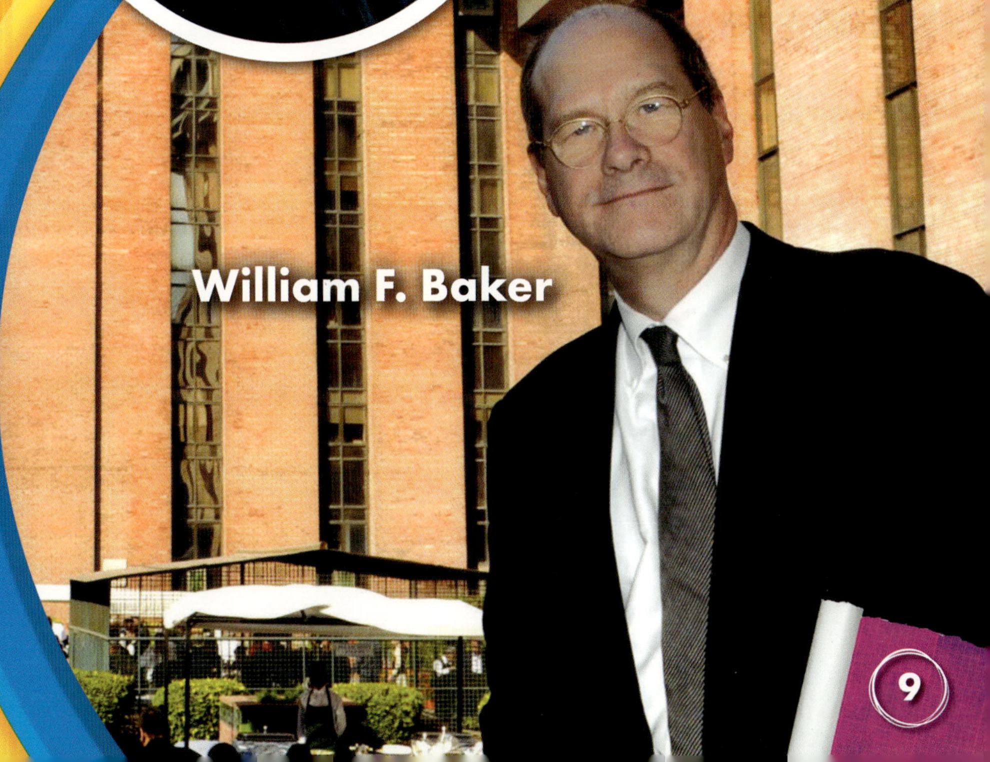

William F. Baker

The tower is made of steel and **concrete**. These make the tower strong. **Piles** support the tower.

Aluminum and glass cover the tower. They protect it from heat and wind.

steel

Machines helped build the tower. Special pumps moved concrete up the tower.

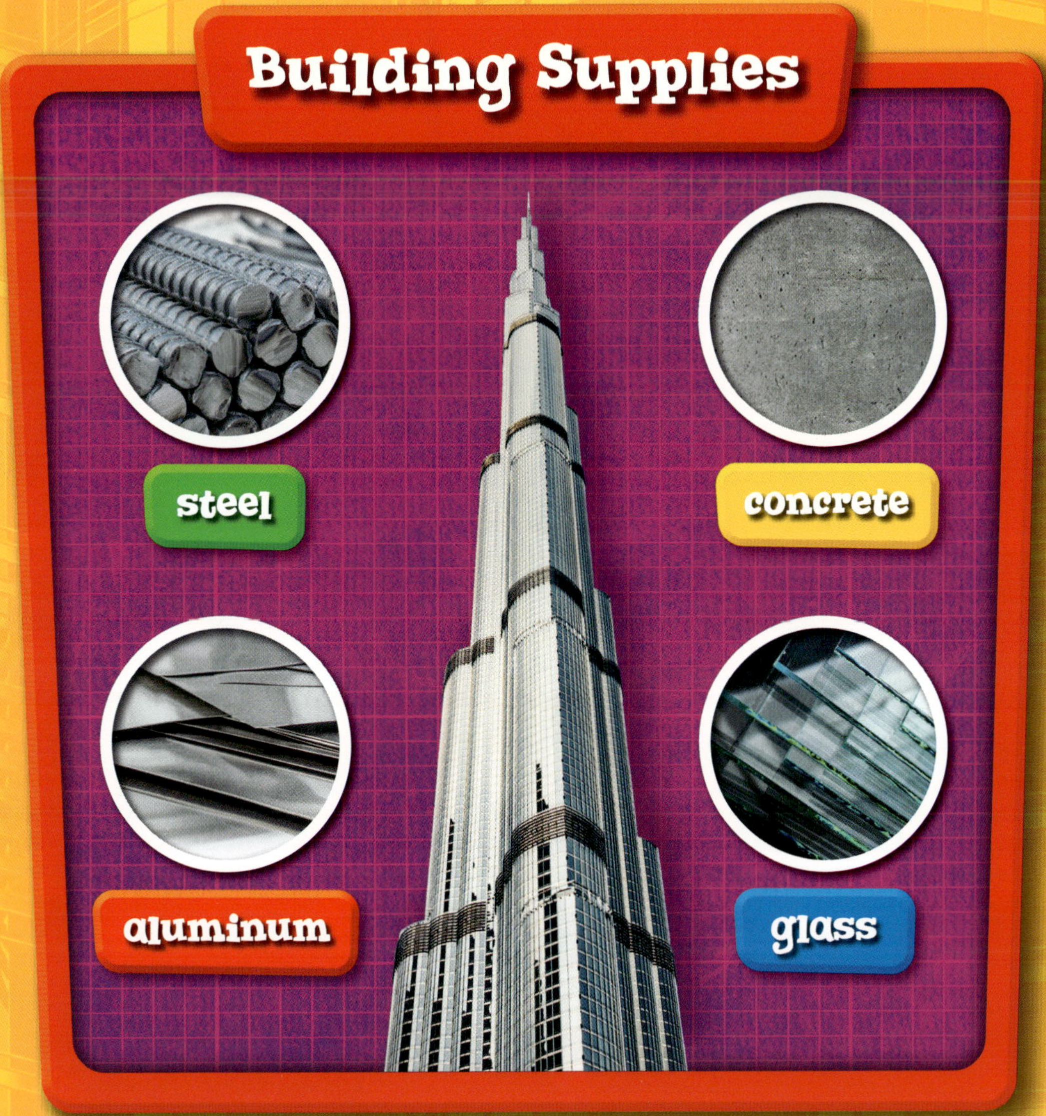

Tower cranes placed the glass and aluminum.

Parts of the Burj Khalifa

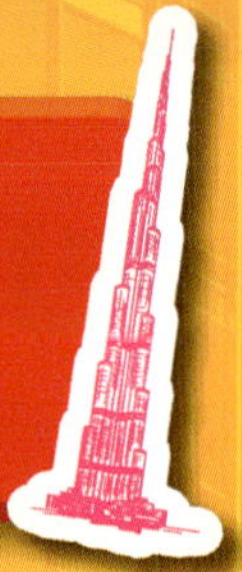

The Burj Khalifa is 2,717 feet (828 meters) tall. It has 163 floors. A **spire** stands on top.

There are three observation decks. The highest one is 1,823 feet (555.7 meters) high!

Super Spire

Height 801 feet (244 meters)

Famous For world's tallest spire as of 2025

The Burj Khalifa has a Y shape.
This makes the tower stable.

Size Comparison

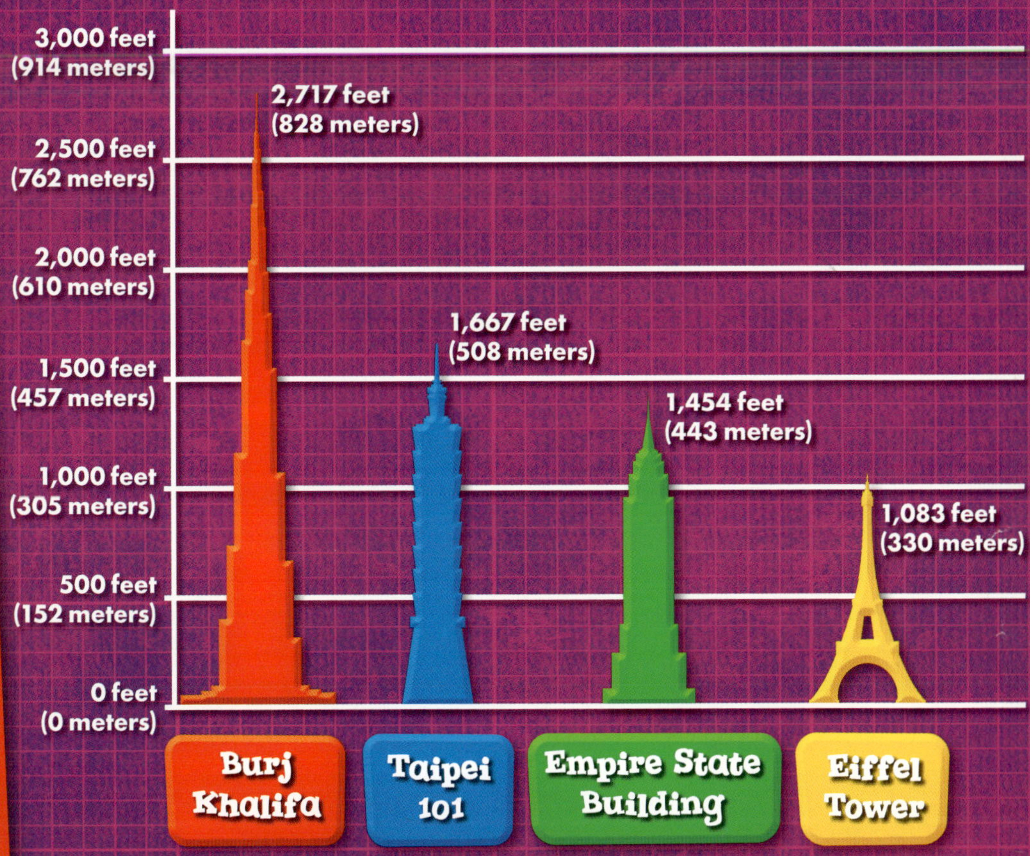

A six-sided core is at the center of the Y. It has elevators. They are very fast.

The Burj Khalifa Today

Many workers help run the Burj Khalifa. Some work at the restaurants. Some fix the elevators. Others keep the building safe.

Many workers clean the tower's windows. They clean over 24,000 windows!

About 17 million visitors see the Burj Khalifa each year. It is one of the most visited landmarks on Earth.

This tower stands tall for all to see!

Glossary

aluminum—a strong, lightweight metal

architect—a person who designs and plans buildings

concrete—a hard, strong building material made with cement, sand, rocks, and water

designed—made a plan for a building, object, or pattern

engineer—a person with science training who designs and builds machines, systems, or structures

observation decks—platforms built so that people can look out at a view

piles—long columns that go into the ground and help support big structures

spire—a pointed structure at the top of a building

tourism—the activity or business of traveling to a place for fun

tower cranes—tall cranes used to lift and move heavy materials to high places